Computerised Accounting Practice Set
Using QuickBooks Online Accounting

Expert Level

This expert level computerised accounting practice set is for students who need to practice exercises of QuickBooks Online Accounting, students can record a month's transactions of Richmond Papers Pty Ltd and can create financial reports.

It covers the following topics.

- Setting Up a New Accounting System
- Suppliers, Purchases and Inventory
- Customers, Sales and Inventory
- Receipts, Payments and Expenses
- Bank Reconciliation
- Financial Reports

Syed Tirmizi
Certified Advisor

ISBN 978-0-9945988-5-1

9 780994 598851 >

Part A
Practice Set

This page is blank.

Instructions

You have recently been appointed as an Accounts Assistant at Richmond Papers Pty Ltd, a new business dealing in printing and publishing. Your responsibilities are to set up a computerised accounting system, update the company records and produce financial reports.

The company started trading on 1st April 2016. All documents have been checked for accuracy and owner of the business, John Smith has authorised these documents.

The company uses straight line method for depreciating its non-current assets at 10% yearly. The policy defines the decline in value of these non-current assets on monthly basis.

You are required to complete the following tasks for April 2016 in the order given.

- a) Setting Up a New Accounting System
- b) Suppliers, Purchases and Inventory
- c) Customers, Sales and Inventory
- d) Receipts, Payments and Expenses
- e) Bank Reconciliation
- f) Financial Reports

a) Setting Up a New Accounting System

Create a new company in QuickBooks Online Accounting using the following information.

Company Name	Richmond Papers Pty Ltd
ABN	46 995 263 632
Address	23 High Street
	Richmond
	VIC 3121
Phone Number	03 9988 7766
Current Financial Year	Jul 2015 – Jun 2016

Set up Suppliers, Customers and Items with the help of Tables 1, 2 and 3.

Additional Information

i. On April 1st 2016, $25,000 Capital was introduced by the owner of the business and was paid into the Bank Current Account. The reference for this transaction is CR0001.

ii. On April 2nd 2016, the Company purchased a motor vehicle from Western Motors for $12,000 + $1,200 GST. Cheque number 000001 was used to make the settlement.

iii. At the end of the month depreciation on the motor vehicle and bank service charges are to be recorded to the relevant accounts.

Table 1: Suppliers

Supplier Account Details	
Contact Name: Sue Hawkins	Email: sales@mt.com.au
Mark & Tony	Telephone: 03 9876 5432
41 Middlesbrough Road	Terms: Net 30
St Albans - VIC 3021	ABN: 84 678 592 583
Contact Name: John Alexander	Email: sales@ds.com.au
David & Sons	Telephone: 03 9765 4321
67 Longwood Road	Terms: Net 30
Craigieburn - VIC 3064	ABN: 65 473 985 624
Contact Name: Angela Samson	Email: sales@ic.com.au
Ian & Co Pty Ltd	Telephone: 03 9654 3210
94 High Street	Terms: Net 30
Fitzroy - VIC 3065	ABN: 25 657 917 634
Contact Name: Andrew Smith	Email: sales@sb.com.au
Smith & Baker	Telephone: 03 9543 2109
11 Westfield Road	Terms: Net 30
Lalor - VIC 3075	ABN: 54 637 945 746
Contact Name: Adam Miller	Email: sales@gc.com.au
Gary Corporation	Telephone: 03 9432 1098
94 Wellington Street	Terms: Net 30
Preston - VIC 3072	ABN: 74 325 496 324
Contact Name: Nick Abbey	Email: sales@ee.com.au
East End Pty Ltd	Telephone: 03 9321 0987
34 Canterbury Road	Terms: Net 30
Epping - VIC 3076	ABN: 96 376 843 587

Table 2: Customers

Customer Account Details	
Contact Name: Megan Boucher Peter Electronics 9 Western Avenue Brooklyn - VIC 3012	Email: info@pe.com.au Telephone: 03 9123 4567 Terms: Net 30 ABN: 52 639 846 324
Contact Name: Ashley Champ Western Estate Agents 362 High Street Sunshine - VIC 3029	Email: info@wea.com.au Telephone: 03 9234 5678 Terms: Net 30 ABN: 47 528 963 764
Contact Name: Natalie Dunn Surf Stores 54 Dundee Street Deer Park - VIC 3023	Email: info@ss.com.au Telephone: 03 9345 6789 Terms: Net 30 ABN: 95 768 359 862
Contact Name: George Gordon Sally's Warehouse 12 Wood Street Essendon - VIC 3040	Email: info@sw.com.au Telephone: 03 9456 7890 Terms: Net 30 ABN: 76 662 485 964
Contact Name: Lee Hopkins Horizon Designs 32 Abbots Road Broadmeadows - VIC 3047	Email: info@hd.com.au Telephone: 03 9567 8901 Terms: Net 30 ABN: 12 528 972 562
Contact Name: Alston Leeson Thomson Clothings 84 Spring Street Thomastown - VIC 3074	Email: info@thc.com.au Telephone: 03 9678 9012 Terms: Net 30 ABN: 74 635 842 321
Contact Name: Robert Nickelson Globe Travels Pty Ltd 42 Barry Road Melbourne - VIC 3000	Email: info@gt.com.au Telephone: 03 9789 0123 Terms: Net 30 ABN: 85 365 412 741
Contact Name: Anthony Robins Tiffany Cakes 36 High Road Williamstown - VIC 3016	Email: info@tc.com.au Telephone: 03 9890 1234 Terms: Net 30 ABN: 78 635 254 524

Table 3: Items

Items Details	
Name & Information: A3 Copy Paper SKU: A3CP Inventory Account: Inventory Asset Inclusive Selling Price: $40	Income Account: Sales - A3 Copy Paper Tax on Sales: GST Expense Account: Purchases - A3 Copy Paper Purchase Tax: GST on non-capital
Name & Information:: A4 Copy Paper SKU: A4CP Inventory Account: Inventory Asset Inclusive Selling Price: $15	Income Account: Sales - A4 Copy Paper Tax on Sales: GST Expense Account: : Purchases - A4 Copy Paper Purchase Tax: GST on non-capital
Name & Information: A5 Copy Paper SKU: A5CP Inventory Account: Inventory Asset Inclusive Selling Price: $14	Income Account: Sales - A5 Copy Paper Tax on Sales: GST Expense Account: : Purchases - A5 Copy Paper Purchase Tax: GST on non-capital
Name & Information: Coloured Paper SKU: COLO Inventory Account: Inventory Asset Inclusive Selling Price: $20	Income Account: Sales - Coloured Paper Tax on Sales: GST Expense Account: : Purchases - Coloured Paper Purchase Tax: GST on non-capital
Name & Information: Envelopes Large SKU: EN01 Inventory Account: Inventory Asset Inclusive Selling Price: $35	Income Account: Sales - Envelopes Large Tax on Sales: GST Expense Account: : Purchases - Envelopes Large Purchase Tax: GST on non-capital
Name & Information: Register Rolls SKU: RR18 Inventory Account: Inventory Asset Inclusive Selling Price: $54	Income Account: Sales - Register Rolls Tax on Sales: GST Expense Account: : Purchases - Register Rolls Purchase Tax: GST on non-capital

b) Suppliers, Purchases and Inventory

Enter the following purchase invoices and purchase returns into the computer.

Purchase Invoices

Date	Supplier	Supp. Inv.	Item	Description	Qty	Cost	Gross Amt Inc GST
April 2nd	Gary Corporation	412	A3CP	A3 Copy Paper	200	$25.00	$5,000.00
April 2nd	Smith & Baker	G/749	A5CP	A5 Copy Paper	250	$8.00	$2,000.00
April 4th	Ian & Co. Pty Ltd	00854	A4CP	A4 Copy Paper	500	$8.00	$4,000.00
April 5th	David & Sons	2016-18	RR18	Register Rolls	350	$38.00	$13,300.00
April 7th	Mark & Tony	A423	COLO	Coloured Paper	200	$14.00	$2,800.00
April 9th	East End Pty Ltd	EE2141	EN01	Envelopes Large	200	$22.00	$4,400.00

Purchase Returns

Date	Supplier	Supp. Inv.	Item	Description	Qty	Cost	Gross Amt Inc GST
April 4th	Smith & Baker	G/749	A5CP	A5 Copy Paper	20	$8.00	$160.00
April 11th	David & Sons	2016-18	RR18	Register Rolls	25	$38.00	$950.00

c) Customers, Sales and Inventory

Enter the following sales invoices and sales returns into the computer.

Sales Invoices

Date	Customer	Doc. No.	Item	Description	Qty	Price	Amount Inc GST
April 5th	Horizon Designs	1001	A4CP	A4 Copy Paper	70	$14.50	$1,015.00
			RR18	Register Rolls	60	$54.00	$3,240.00
			A5CP	A5 Copy Paper	70	$14.00	$980.00
						Total	$5,235.00
April 10th	Thomson Clothings	1002	A4CP	A4 Copy Paper	60	$15.00	$900.00
			EN01	Envelopes Large	80	$35.00	$2,800.00
						Total	$3,700.00
April 12th	Globe Travels Pty Ltd	1003	A4CP	A4 Copy Paper	60	$15.00	$900.00
			A3CP	A3 Copy Paper	50	$40.00	$2,000.00
			RR18	Register Rolls	70	$54.00	$3,780.00
			COLO	Coloured Paper	60	$20.00	$1,200.00
						Total	$7,880.00
April 14th	Tiffany Cakes	1004	A4CP	A4 Copy Paper	50	$15.00	$750.00
			RR18	Register Rolls	60	$54.00	$3,240.00
			EN01	Envelopes Large	60	$35.00	$2,100.00
						Total	$6,090.00
April 19th	Peter Electronics	1005	A4CP	A4 Copy Paper	60	$15.00	$900.00
			COLO	Coloured Paper	70	$20.00	$1,400.00
						Total	$2,300.00
April 21st	Sally's Warehouse	1006	A4CP	A4 Copy Paper	70	$15.00	$1,050.00
			COLO	Coloured Paper	60	$20.00	$1,200.00
			A3CP	A3 Copy Paper	70	$40.00	$2,800.00
			RR18	Register Rolls	50	$54.00	$2,700.00
						Total	$7,750.00
April 25th	Western Estate Agents	1007	A5CP	A5 Copy Paper	100	$14.00	$1,400.00
						Total	$1,400.00
April 27th	Surf Stores	1008	A4CP	A4 Copy Paper	50	$15.00	$750.00
			RR18	Register Rolls	30	$54.00	$1,620.00
						Total	$2,370.00

Sales Returns

Date	Customer	Doc. No.	Item	Description	Qty	Price	Amount Inc GST
April 17th	Thomson Clothings	1009	EN01	Envelopes Large	20	$35.00	$700.00
April 23rd	Sally's Warehouse	1010	A4CP	A4 Copy Paper	10	$15.00	$150.00

d) Receipts, Payments and Expenses

Enter the following payments received from customers, payments made to suppliers and expenses into the computer.

Payments Received

Date	Receipt Type	Customer	Details	Amount ($)
April 13th	EFT	Horizon Designs	Invoice 1001	$5,235.00
April 18th	Cheque	Thomson Clothings	Invoice 1002	$3,000.00
April 20th	Cheque	Globe Travels Ltd	Invoice 1003	$7,880.00
April 25th	EFT	Tiffany Cakes	Invoice 1004	$6,090.00

Expenses Summary

Date	Cheque No.	Expenses	Details	Net	Tax	Gross ($)
April 2nd	000002	Rent	Richmond Real Estate	$1,000.00	$100.00	$1,100.00
April 7th	000003	Insurance Premium	Melbourne Insurance	$200.00	$20.00	$220.00
April 19th	000004	Electricity Bill	Victoria Electricity	$176.73	$17.67	$194.40
April 21st	000005	Telephone Bill	Australia Telecom	$196.92	$19.62	$215.84
April 26th	000006	Cleaning	Melbourne Removals	$50.00	$5.00	$55.00

Payments Made

Date	Cheque No.	Supplier	Details	Amount ($)
April 28th	000007	Gary Corporation	412	$5,000.00
April 28th	000008	Smith & Baker	G/749	$1,840.00

e) Bank Reconciliation

Prepare bank reconciliation for the month of April 2016. Company bank statement is as follows.

	BANK OF RICHMOND				
	36 Spring Street, Richmond, VIC 3121		**Cheque Account Statement**		
	TEL 1800 AUSTRALIA		30-04-2016		

Richmond Papers Pty Ltd	**BSB Number**	**Account Number**
23 High Street	123-456	987654321
Richmond		
VIC 3121		

Date	Details	Ref	Withdrawal	Deposits	Balance
01-Apr-16	Account opened - Initial deposit			$25,000.00	$25,000.00
02-Apr-16	CHQ 000001		$13,200.00		$11,800.00
02-Apr-16	CHQ 000002		$1,100.00		$10,700.00
07-Apr-16	CHQ 000003		$220.00		$10,480.00
13-Apr-16	EFT – Horizon Designs			$5,235.00	$15,715.00
18-Apr-16	Cheque deposited			$3,000.00	$18,715.00
19-Apr-16	CHQ 000004		$194.40		$18,520.60
20-Apr-16	Cheque deposited			$7,880.00	$26,400.60
21-Apr-16	CHQ 000005		$215.84		$26,184.76
22-Apr-16	CHQ 000007		$5,000.00		$21,184.76
25-Apr-16	EFT – Tiffany Cakes			$6,090.00	$27,274.76
30-Apr-16	Bank charges		$10.00		$27,264.76
	Totals		**$19,930.24**	**$47,205.00**	

f) Financial Reports

Print or save the following reports for the month of April 2016.

     I.   A/P Ageing Summary

    II.   A/R Ageing Summary

   III.   Item Valuation Detail

  IV.   Purchases by Product/Service Detail

    V.   Sales by Product/Service Detail

  VI.   Invoice List by Date

 VII.   Cheque Detail

VIII.   Bank Reconciliation Report

  IX.   Statement of Cash Flows

   X.   Trial Balance Report

  XI.   Profit and Loss Report

 XII.   Balance Sheet Report

Part B

Solutions

This page is blank.

Richmond Papers Pty Ltd
A/P AGEING SUMMARY
As of April 30, 2016

	CURRENT	1 - 30	31 - 60	61 - 90	91 AND OVER	TOTAL
David & Sons	13,300.00	-950.00				A$12,350.00
East End Pty Ltd	4,400.00					A$4,400.00
Ian & Co Pty Ltd	4,000.00					A$4,000.00
Mark & Tony	2,800.00					A$2,800.00
TOTAL	A$24,500.00	A$ -950.00	A$0.00	A$0.00	A$0.00	A$23,550.00

Richmond Papers Pty Ltd
A/R AGEING SUMMARY
As of April 30, 2016

	CURRENT	1 - 30	31 - 60	61 - 90	91 AND OVER	TOTAL
Peter Electronics	2,300.00					A$2,300.00
Sally's Warehouse	7,750.00	-150.00				A$7,600.00
Surf Stores	2,370.00					A$2,370.00
Thomson Clothings	700.00	-700.00				A$0.00
Western Estate Agents	1,400.00					A$1,400.00
TOTAL	A$14,520.00	A$ -850.00	A$0.00	A$0.00	A$0.00	A$13,670.00

Richmond Papers Pty Ltd
INVENTORY VALUATION DETAIL
April 2016

DATE	TRANSACTION TYPE	NO.	QTY	QUANTITY	AVG COST	UNIT PRICE/RATE	ASSET VALUE
A3 Copy Paper							
01/04/2016	Inventory Starting Value	START	0.00	0.00	0.00		0.00
02/04/2016	Bill	412	200.00	200.00	22.73	22.72725	4,545.45
10/04/2016	Invoice	1003	-50.00	150.00	22.73	22.72725	3,409.09
21/04/2016	Invoice	1006	-70.00	80.00	22.73	22.72725	1,818.18
A4 Copy Paper							
01/04/2016	Inventory Starting Value	START	0.00	0.00	0.00		0.00
04/04/2016	Bill	00854	500.00	500.00	7.27	7.27272	3,636.36
05/04/2016	Invoice	1001	-70.00	430.00	7.27	7.27272	3,127.27
10/04/2016	Invoice	1003	-60.00	370.00	7.27	7.27272	2,690.91
10/04/2016	Invoice	1002	-60.00	310.00	7.27	7.27272	2,254.55
14/04/2016	Invoice	1004	-50.00	260.00	7.27	7.27272	1,890.91
19/04/2016	Invoice	1005	-60.00	200.00	7.27	7.27272	1,454.55
21/04/2016	Invoice	1006	-70.00	130.00	7.27	7.27272	945.46
23/04/2016	Adjustment Note	1010	10.00	140.00	7.27	7.27272	1,018.19
27/04/2016	Invoice	1008	-50.00	90.00	7.27	7.27272	654.55
A5 Copy Paper							
01/04/2016	Inventory Starting Value	START	0.00	0.00	0.00		0.00
02/04/2016	Bill	G/749	250.00	250.00	7.27	7.27272	1,818.18
04/04/2016	Supplier Credit	G/749	-20.00	230.00	7.27	7.2725	1,672.73
04/04/2016	Supplier Credit	G/749	0.00	230.00	7.27	-0.00022	1,672.73
05/04/2016	Invoice	1001	-70.00	160.00	7.27	7.27272	1,163.64
25/04/2016	Invoice	1007	-100.00	60.00	7.27	7.27272	436.37
Coloured Paper							
01/04/2016	Inventory Starting Value	START	0.00	0.00	0.00		0.00
07/04/2016	Bill	A423	200.00	200.00	12.73	12.72725	2,545.45
10/04/2016	Invoice	1003	-60.00	140.00	12.73	12.72725	1,781.81
19/04/2016	Invoice	1005	-70.00	70.00	12.73	12.72725	890.90
21/04/2016	Invoice	1006	-60.00	10.00	12.73	12.72725	127.26
Envelopes Large							
01/04/2016	Inventory Starting Value	START	0.00	0.00	0.00	15.00	0.00
09/04/2016	Bill	EE2141	200.00	200.00	20.00	20.00	4,000.00
10/04/2016	Invoice	1002	-80.00	120.00	20.00	20.00	2,400.00
14/04/2016	Invoice	1004	-60.00	60.00	20.00	20.00	1,200.00
17/04/2016	Adjustment Note	1009	20.00	80.00	20.00	20.00	1,600.00
Register Rolls							
01/04/2016	Inventory Starting Value	START	0.00	0.00	0.00		0.00
05/04/2016	Bill	2016-18	350.00	350.00	34.55	34.5454571	12,090.91
05/04/2016	Invoice	1001	-60.00	290.00	34.55	34.5454571	10,018.18
10/04/2016	Invoice	1003	-70.00	220.00	34.55	34.5454571	7,600.00
11/04/2016	Supplier Credit	2016-18	-25.00	195.00	34.55	34.5456	6,736.36
11/04/2016	Supplier Credit	2016-18	0.00	195.00	34.55	0.0001429	6,736.36
14/04/2016	Invoice	1004	-60.00	135.00	34.55	34.5454571	4,663.63
21/04/2016	Invoice	1006	-50.00	85.00	34.55	34.5454571	2,936.36
27/04/2016	Invoice	1008	-30.00	55.00	34.55	34.5454571	1,900.00

Richmond Papers Pty Ltd
PURCHASES BY PRODUCT/SERVICE DETAIL
April 2016

DATE	TRANSACTION TYPE	NO.	SUPPLIER	MEMO/DESCRIPTION	QTY	UNIT PRICE/RATE	BALANCE
A3 Copy Paper							
01/04/2016	Inventory Starting Value	START		A3CP - Opening inventory and value	0.00		0.00
02/04/2016	Bill	412	Gary Corporation	A3 Copy Paper	200.00	22.72725	4,545.45
A4 Copy Paper							
01/04/2016	Inventory Starting Value	START		A4CP - Opening inventory and value	0.00		0.00
04/04/2016	Bill	00854	Ian & Co Pty Ltd	A4 Copy Paper	500.00	7.27272	3,636.36
A5 Copy Paper							
01/04/2016	Inventory Starting Value	START		A5CP - Opening inventory and value	0.00		0.00
02/04/2016	Bill	G/749	Smith & Baker	A5 Copy Paper	250.00	7.27272	1,818.18
04/04/2016	Supplier Credit	G/749	Smith & Baker	A5 Copy Paper	20.00	-0.00022	1,818.18
04/04/2016	Supplier Credit	G/749	Smith & Baker	A5 Copy Paper	-20.00	7.2725	1,672.73
04/04/2016	Supplier Credit	G/749	Smith & Baker	A5 Copy Paper	-20.00	-0.00022	1,672.73
Coloured Paper							
01/04/2016	Inventory Starting Value	START		A3 Copy Papers - Opening inventory and value	0.00		0.00
07/04/2016	Bill	A423	Mark & Tony	Coloured Paper	200.00	12.72725	2,545.45
Envelopes Large							
01/04/2016	Inventory Starting Value	START		A Copy Paper - Opening inventory and value	0.00	15.00	0.00
09/04/2016	Bill	EE2141	East End Pty Ltd	Envelopes Large	200.00	20.00	4,000.00
Register Rolls							
01/04/2016	Inventory Starting Value	START		Register Rolls - Opening inventory and value	0.00		0.00
05/04/2016	Bill	2016-18	David & Sons	Register Rolls	350.00	34.5454571	12,090.91
11/04/2016	Supplier Credit	2016-18	David & Sons	Register Rolls	-25.00	34.5456	11,227.27
11/04/2016	Supplier Credit	2016-18	David & Sons	Register Rolls	25.00	0.0001429	11,227.27
11/04/2016	Supplier Credit	2016-18	David & Sons	Register Rolls	-25.00	0.0001429	11,227.27

TOTAL

Accruals Basis

Richmond Papers Pty Ltd
SALES BY PRODUCT/SERVICE DETAIL
April 2016

DATE	TRANSACTION TYPE	NO.	CLIENT	MEMO/DESCRIPTION	QTY	UNIT PRICE/RATE	AMOUNT	BALANCE
A3 Copy Paper								
10/04/2016	Invoice	1003	Globe Travels Pty Ltd	A3 Copy Paper	50.00	36.3636	1,818.18	1,818.18
10/04/2016	Invoice	1003	Globe Travels Pty Ltd	A3 Copy Paper	-50.00	22.72725	-1,136.36	681.82
10/04/2016	Invoice	1003	Globe Travels Pty Ltd	A3 Copy Paper	50.00	22.72725	1,136.36	1,818.18
21/04/2016	Invoice	1006	Sally's Warehouse	A3 Copy Paper	70.00	22.72725	1,590.91	3,409.09
21/04/2016	Invoice	1006	Sally's Warehouse	A3 Copy Paper	70.00	36.3635714	2,545.45	5,954.54
21/04/2016	Invoice	1006	Sally's Warehouse	A3 Copy Paper	-70.00	22.72725	-1,590.91	4,363.63
Total for A3 Copy Paper							**A$4,363.63**	
A4 Copy Paper								
05/04/2016	Invoice	1001	Horizon Designs	A4 Copy Paper	-70.00	7.27272	-509.09	-509.09
05/04/2016	Invoice	1001	Horizon Designs	A4 Copy Paper	70.00	13.1818571	922.73	413.64
05/04/2016	Invoice	1001	Horizon Designs	A4 Copy Paper	70.00	7.27272	509.09	922.73
10/04/2016	Invoice	1002	Thomson Clothings	A4 Copy Paper	-60.00	7.27272	-436.36	486.37
10/04/2016	Invoice	1002	Thomson Clothings	A4 Copy Paper	60.00	13.6363333	818.18	1,304.55
10/04/2016	Invoice	1003	Globe Travels Pty Ltd	A4 Copy Paper	60.00	7.27272	436.36	1,740.91
10/04/2016	Invoice	1002	Thomson Clothings	A4 Copy Paper	60.00	7.27272	436.36	2,177.27
10/04/2016	Invoice	1003	Globe Travels Pty Ltd	A4 Copy Paper	-60.00	7.27272	-436.36	1,740.91
10/04/2016	Invoice	1003	Globe Travels Pty Ltd	A4 Copy Paper	60.00	13.6363333	818.18	2,559.09
14/04/2016	Invoice	1004	Tiffany Cakes	A4 Copy Paper	50.00	7.27272	363.64	2,922.73
14/04/2016	Invoice	1004	Tiffany Cakes	A4 Copy Paper	50.00	13.6364	681.82	3,604.55
14/04/2016	Invoice	1004	Tiffany Cakes	A4 Copy Paper	-50.00	7.27272	-363.64	3,240.91
19/04/2016	Invoice	1005	Peter Electronics	A4 Copy Paper	-60.00	7.27272	-436.36	2,804.55
19/04/2016	Invoice	1005	Peter Electronics	A4 Copy Paper	60.00	7.27272	436.36	3,240.91
19/04/2016	Invoice	1005	Peter Electronics	A4 Copy Paper	60.00	13.6363333	818.18	4,059.09
21/04/2016	Invoice	1006	Sally's Warehouse	A4 Copy Paper	-70.00	7.27272	-509.09	3,550.00
21/04/2016	Invoice	1006	Sally's Warehouse	A4 Copy Paper	70.00	13.6364286	954.55	4,504.55
21/04/2016	Invoice	1006	Sally's Warehouse	A4 Copy Paper	70.00	7.27272	509.09	5,013.64
23/04/2016	Adjustment Note	1010	Sally's Warehouse	A4 Copy Paper	-10.00	7.27272	-72.73	4,940.91
23/04/2016	Adjustment Note	1010	Sally's Warehouse	A4 Copy Paper	-10.00	13.636	-136.36	4,804.55
23/04/2016	Adjustment Note	1010	Sally's Warehouse	A4 Copy Paper	10.00	7.27272	72.73	4,877.28
27/04/2016	Invoice	1008	Surf Stores	A4 Copy Paper	50.00	13.6364	681.82	5,559.10
27/04/2016	Invoice	1008	Surf Stores	A4 Copy Paper	-50.00	7.27272	-363.64	5,195.46
27/04/2016	Invoice	1008	Surf Stores	A4 Copy Paper	50.00	7.27272	363.64	5,559.10
Total for A4 Copy Paper							**A$5,559.10**	

A5 Copy Paper

05/04/2016	Invoice	1001	Horizon Designs	A5 Copy Paper	70.00	12.7272857	890.91	890.91
05/04/2016	Invoice	1001	Horizon Designs	A5 Copy Paper	70.00	7.27272	509.09	1,400.00
05/04/2016	Invoice	1001	Horizon Designs	A5 Copy Paper	-70.00	7.27272	-509.09	890.91
25/04/2016	Invoice	1007	Western Estate Agents	A5 Copy Paper	100.00	12.7273	1,272.73	2,163.64
25/04/2016	Invoice	1007	Western Estate Agents	A5 Copy Paper	-100.00	7.27272	-727.27	1,436.37
25/04/2016	Invoice	1007	Western Estate Agents	A5 Copy Paper	100.00	7.27272	727.27	2,163.64

Total for A5 Copy Paper — A$2,163.64

Coloured Paper

10/04/2016	Invoice	1003	Globe Travels Pty Ltd	Coloured Paper	60.00	12.72725	763.64	763.64
10/04/2016	Invoice	1003	Globe Travels Pty Ltd	Coloured Paper	60.00	18.1818333	1,090.91	1,854.55
10/04/2016	Invoice	1003	Globe Travels Pty Ltd	Coloured Paper	-60.00	12.72725	-763.64	1,090.91
19/04/2016	Invoice	1005	Peter Electronics	Coloured Paper	-70.00	12.72725	-890.91	200.00
19/04/2016	Invoice	1005	Peter Electronics	Coloured Paper	70.00	18.1818571	1,272.73	1,472.73
19/04/2016	Invoice	1005	Peter Electronics	Coloured Paper	70.00	12.72725	890.91	2,363.64
21/04/2016	Invoice	1006	Sally's Warehouse	Coloured Paper	60.00	18.1818333	1,090.91	3,454.55
21/04/2016	Invoice	1006	Sally's Warehouse	Coloured Paper	-60.00	12.72725	-763.64	2,690.91
21/04/2016	Invoice	1006	Sally's Warehouse	Coloured Paper	60.00	12.72725	763.64	3,454.55

Total for Coloured Paper — A$3,454.55

Envelopes Large

10/04/2016	Invoice	1002	Thomson Clothings	Envelopes Large	80.00	20.00	1,600.00	1,600.00
10/04/2016	Invoice	1002	Thomson Clothings	Envelopes Large	-80.00	20.00	-1,600.00	0.00
10/04/2016	Invoice	1002	Thomson Clothings	Envelopes Large	80.00	31.818125	2,545.45	2,545.45
14/04/2016	Invoice	1004	Tiffany Cakes	Envelopes Large	60.00	31.8181667	1,909.09	4,454.54
14/04/2016	Invoice	1004	Tiffany Cakes	Envelopes Large	60.00	20.00	1,200.00	5,654.54
14/04/2016	Invoice	1004	Tiffany Cakes	Envelopes Large	-60.00	20.00	-1,200.00	4,454.54
17/04/2016	Adjustment Note	1009	Thomson Clothings	Envelopes Large	20.00	20.00	400.00	4,854.54
17/04/2016	Adjustment Note	1009	Thomson Clothings	Envelopes Large	-20.00	31.818	-636.36	4,218.18
17/04/2016	Adjustment Note	1009	Thomson Clothings	Envelopes Large	-20.00	20.00	-400.00	3,818.18

Total for Envelopes Large — A$3,818.18

Register Rolls

05/04/2016	Invoice	1001	Horizon Designs	Register Rolls	60.00	34.5454571	2,072.73	2,072.73
05/04/2016	Invoice	1001	Horizon Designs	Register Rolls	60.00	49.0908333	2,945.45	5,018.18
05/04/2016	Invoice	1001	Horizon Designs	Register Rolls	-60.00	34.5454571	-2,072.73	2,945.45
10/04/2016	Invoice	1003	Globe Travels Pty Ltd	Register Rolls	70.00	34.5454571	2,418.18	5,363.63
10/04/2016	Invoice	1003	Globe Travels Pty Ltd	Register Rolls	70.00	49.0908571	3,436.36	8,799.99
10/04/2016	Invoice	1003	Globe	Register Rolls	-70.00	34.5454571	-2,418.18	6,381.81

			Travels Pty Ltd					
14/04/2016	Invoice	1004	Tiffany Cakes	Register Rolls	60.00	49.0908333	2,945.45	9,327.26
14/04/2016	Invoice	1004	Tiffany Cakes	Register Rolls	60.00	34.5454571	2,072.73	11,399.99
14/04/2016	Invoice	1004	Tiffany Cakes	Register Rolls	-60.00	34.5454571	-2,072.73	9,327.26
21/04/2016	Invoice	1006	Sally's Warehouse	Register Rolls	-50.00	34.5454571	-1,727.27	7,599.99
21/04/2016	Invoice	1006	Sally's Warehouse	Register Rolls	50.00	34.5454571	1,727.27	9,327.26
21/04/2016	Invoice	1006	Sally's Warehouse	Register Rolls	50.00	49.091	2,454.55	11,781.81
27/04/2016	Invoice	1008	Surf Stores	Register Rolls	-30.00	34.5454571	-1,036.36	10,745.45
27/04/2016	Invoice	1008	Surf Stores	Register Rolls	30.00	34.5454571	1,036.36	11,781.81
27/04/2016	Invoice	1008	Surf Stores	Register Rolls	30.00	49.091	1,472.73	13,254.54
Total for Register Rolls							**A$13,254.54**	
TOTAL							**A$32,613.64**	

Accruals Basis

Richmond Papers Pty Ltd
INVOICE LIST BY DATE
April 2016

DATE	TRANSACTION TYPE	NO.	NAME	MEMO/DESCRIPTION	DUE DATE	AMOUNT	OPEN BALANCE
05/04/2016	Invoice	1001	Horizon Designs		05/05/2016	5,235.00	0.00
10/04/2016	Invoice	1002	Thomson Clothings		10/05/2016	3,700.00	700.00
10/04/2016	Invoice	1003	Globe Travels Pty Ltd		10/05/2016	7,880.00	0.00
14/04/2016	Invoice	1004	Tiffany Cakes		14/05/2016	6,090.00	0.00
19/04/2016	Invoice	1005	Peter Electronics		19/05/2016	2,300.00	2,300.00
21/04/2016	Invoice	1006	Sally's Warehouse		21/05/2016	7,750.00	7,750.00
25/04/2016	Invoice	1007	Western Estate Agents		25/05/2016	1,400.00	1,400.00
27/04/2016	Invoice	1008	Surf Stores		27/05/2016	2,370.00	2,370.00

Richmond Papers Pty Ltd
CHEQUE DETAIL
April 2016

DATE	TRANSACTION TYPE	NO.	NAME	MEMO/DESCRIPTION	CLR	AMOUNT
Bank of Richmond						
02/04/2016	Expense	000001	Western Motors		R	-13,200.00
				Motor vehicle purchased		12,000.00
						-1,200.00
02/04/2016	Expense	000002	Richmond Real Estate		R	-1,100.00
				Rent		1,000.00
						-100.00
07/04/2016	Expense	000003	Melbourne Insurance		R	-220.00
				Insurance		200.00
						-20.00
19/04/2016	Expense	000004	Victoria Electricity		R	-194.40
				Electricity		176.73
						-17.67
21/04/2016	Expense	000005	Australia Telecom		R	-215.84
				Telephone		196.22
						-19.62
28/04/2016	Expense	000006	Melbourne Removals			-55.00
				Cleaning		50.00
						-5.00
28/04/2016	Bill Payment (Cheque)	000007	Gary Corporation		R	-5,000.00
						-5,000.00
28/04/2016	Bill Payment (Cheque)	000008	Smith & Baker			-1,840.00
						-1,840.00
30/04/2016	Cheque Expense	SVCCHRG		Service Charge	R	-10.00
						10.00

Richmond Papers Pty Ltd
Reconciliation Report
Bank of Richmond, Period Ending 30/04/2016
Reconciled on: 15/05/2016 (any changes to transactions after this date aren't reflected on this report)
Reconciled by: Syed Tirmizi

Summary

Statement Beginning Balance	0.00
Cheques and Payments cleared	-19,940.24
Deposits and Other Credits cleared	+47,205.00
Statement Ending Balance	27,264.76
Uncleared transactions as of 30/04/2016	-1,895.00
Register Balance as of 30/04/2016	25,369.76

Details

Cheques and Payments cleared

Date	Type	No.	Name	Amount
02/04/2016	Expense	000001		-13,200.00
02/04/2016	Expense	000002	Richmond Real Estate	-1,100.00
07/04/2016	Expense	000003	Melbourne Insurance	-220.00
19/04/2016	Expense	000004	Victoria Electricity	-194.40
21/04/2016	Expense	000005	Australia Telecom	-215.84
28/04/2016	Bill Payment	000007	Gary Corporation	-5,000.00
30/04/2016	Cheque Expense	SVCCHRG		-10.00

Total				-19,940.24

Deposits and Other Credits cleared

Date	Type	No.	Name	Amount
01/04/2016	Deposit			25,000.00
13/04/2016	Payment	Invoice 1001	Horizon Designs	5,235.00
18/04/2016	Payment	Invoice 1002	Thomson Clothings	3,000.00
20/04/2016	Payment	Invoice 1003	Globe Travels Pty Ltd	7,880.00
25/04/2016	Payment	Invoice 1004	Tiffany Cakes	6,090.00

Total				47,205.00

Additional Information

Uncleared Cheques and Payments as of 30/04/2016

Date	Type	No.	Name	Amount
28/04/2016	Expense	000006	Melbourne Removals	-55.00
28/04/2016	Bill Payment	000008	Smith & Baker	-1,840.00

Total				-1,895.00

Richmond Papers Pty Ltd
STATEMENT OF CASH FLOWS
April 2016

	TOTAL
Cash flows from operating activities	
Profit for the year	9,789.79
Adjustments for non-cash income and expenses:	
Accounts receivable	-13,670.00
Inventory Asset	-6,536.36
Accumulated depreciation on motor vehicles	100.00
Accounts payable	23,550.00
BAS Liabilities Payable	-863.67
Total Adjustments for non-cash income and expenses:	2,579.97
Net cash from operating activities	A$12,369.76
Cash flows from investing activities	
Motor vehicles	-12,000.00
Net cash used in investing activities	A$ -12,000.00
Cash flows from financing activities	
Owner's Equity	25,000.00
Net cash used in financing activities	A$25,000.00
Net increase (decrease) in cash and cash equivalents	A$25,369.76
Cash and cash equivalents at end of year	A$25,369.76

Richmond Papers Pty Ltd
TRIAL BALANCE
As of April 30, 2016

	DEBIT	CREDIT
Bank of Richmond	25,369.76	
Accounts receivable	13,670.00	
Inventory Asset	6,536.36	
Accumulated depreciation on motor vehicles		100.00
Motor vehicles	12,000.00	
Accounts payable		23,550.00
BAS Liabilities Payable	863.67	
Owner's Equity		25,000.00
Sales - A3 Copy Paper		4,363.63
Sales - A4 Copy Paper		5,559.10
Sales - A5 Copy Paper		2,163.64
Sales - Coloured Paper		3,454.55
Sales - Envelopes Large		3,818.18
Sales - Register Rolls		13,254.54
Purchases - A3 Copy Paper	2,727.27	
Purchases - A4 Copy Paper	2,981.81	
Purchases - A5 Copy Paper	1,236.36	
Purchases - Coloured Paper	2,418.19	
Purchases - Envelopes Large	2,400.00	
Purchases - Register Rolls	9,327.27	
Bank charges	10.00	
Cleaning	50.00	
Electricity	176.73	
Insurance expenses	200.00	
Motor vehicle expenses	100.00	
Rent or lease payments	1,000.00	
Telephone & internet expenses	196.22	
TOTAL	A$81,263.64	A$81,263.64

Accruals Basis

Richmond Papers Pty Ltd
PROFIT AND LOSS
April 2016

	TOTAL
Income	
Sales - A3 Copy Paper	4,363.63
Sales - A4 Copy Paper	5,559.10
Sales - A5 Copy Paper	2,163.64
Sales - Coloured Paper	3,454.55
Sales - Envelopes Large	3,818.18
Sales - Register Rolls	13,254.54
Total Income	**A$32,613.64**
Cost of Sales	
Purchases - A3 Copy Paper	2,727.27
Purchases - A4 Copy Paper	2,981.81
Purchases - A5 Copy Paper	1,236.36
Purchases - Coloured Paper	2,418.19
Purchases - Envelopes Large	2,400.00
Purchases - Register Rolls	9,327.27
Total Cost of Sales	**A$21,090.90**
Gross Profit	**A$11,522.74**
Expenses	
Bank charges	10.00
Cleaning	50.00
Electricity	176.73
Insurance expenses	200.00
Motor vehicle expenses	100.00
Rent or lease payments	1,000.00
Telephone & internet expenses	196.22
Total Expenses	**A$1,732.95**
Net Earnings	**A$9,789.79**

Accruals Basis

Richmond Papers Pty Ltd
BALANCE SHEET
As of April 30, 2016

	TOTAL
Assets	
Current Assets	
Accounts receivable	
Accounts receivable	13,670.00
Total Accounts receivable	A$13,670.00
Bank of Richmond	25,369.76
Inventory Asset	6,536.36
Total Current Assets	A$45,576.12
Long-term assets	
Accumulated depreciation on motor vehicles	-100.00
Motor vehicles	12,000.00
Total long-term assets	11,900.00
Total Assets	A$57,476.12
Liabilities and shareholder's equity	
Current liabilities:	
Accounts payable	
Accounts payable	23,550.00
Total Accounts payable	A$23,550.00
BAS Liabilities Payable	-863.67
Total current liabilities	A$22,686.33
Shareholders' equity:	
Net Income	9,789.79
Owner's Equity	25,000.00
Retained Earnings	
Total shareholders' equity	A$34,789.79
Total liabilities and equity	A$57,476.12

Accruals Basis